# Preface

Over the past many years, I have been researching artificial intelligence (AI) and in particular, its potential use in healthcare. I have observed the hype in the media as to how AI will replace clinicians. On the other hand, I have heard many health practitioners dismiss AI as another technological fad soon to see its demise. However, if one were to adopt a balanced and well-informed view, it would be easy to see where the limitations of AI are and where its potential for application in healthcare. As health systems face rising costs of healthcare delivery and clinicians face challenges of absorbing expanding medical information and meeting the demands of patients, AI holds great potential in addressing these issues. A sensible approach to using AI that ensures the interests of patients will definitely change the way healthcare is currently delivered. In this book, I have compiled all the articles I have penned, which track the progress of AI in Healthcare from theory to application. I hope this book not only can introduce interested readers to the promise of AI in Healthcare but also provide a sensible perspective as to what AI can mean for healthcare.

*Sandeep*

# Contents

# The Context

# Chapter 1: Where would AI make the greatest impact?

Of all the sectors that Artificial Intelligence (AI) is to have an impact, it will be the most significant in healthcare. Why so? Healthcare delivery because of the processes involved in detecting, managing and treating diseases involves a complex approach. This complex approach requires collaboration not just between professionals or medical disciplines but also between providers and beneficiaries. This collaboration is unlike many other sectors.

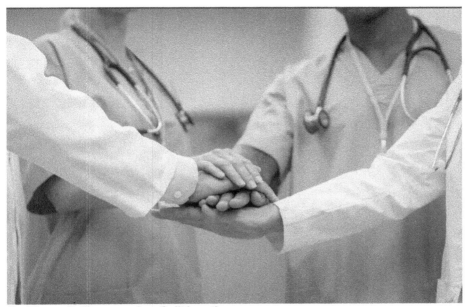

*Healthcare Delivery requires Collaboration*

However, achieving this collaboration is not easy and can be costly. Medicine has become increasingly specialized over the years leading to compartmentalization of healthcare delivery. Where collaboration is necessary, it is not occurring. Further, the importance accorded to the end product (health) means that investment in the sector is relatively higher compared to many other sectors.

These combinations of factors have meant healthcare is ripe for disruption or at the least in need for operational and financial efficiency measures. Technology (whether it is AI, Genomics, VR, AR, Blockchain, Digital Infrastructure, Robotics. Etc) is set to play a big role in this disruption. Tech companies that haven't been traditionally involved in healthcare delivery are now seeing the value of introducing technology in healthcare and heavily investing in this sector.

Of all the technological innovations being used or trialled in healthcare delivery, I strongly believe AI (I include machine learning/deep learning and robotics here) will have the greatest disruptive factor. Yes, genomics and digital health will have a great impact, but they are set-up to integrate into traditional care models rather than be disruptive. I have to clarify here when I use 'disruptive', it doesn't mean total replacement of clinicians nor how patients perceive health as a product, but it relates to how and where medical treatment is delivered. To explain this, let me start with a basic component of healthcare delivery: medical workforce. While governments and private players continue to invest in medical training, the increasing demand for healthcare and the time taken to train medical doctors has meant shortages of doctors continue to persist. In some places, it is all the more acute (see below figure).

# Will there be enough doctors?

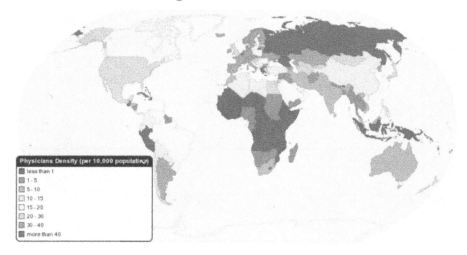

*Doctor Density across the World (Source: CB Insights, 2019)*

From a patient's perspective, all things being ideal, they should be able to pick the doctor or health service they require at the location and time of their choosing. However, because of reasons that are too complex to cover in this current article, this doesn't occur in reality. In developing countries, there isn't even a choice with absence of health services and doctors in many rural locations. In these situations, any form of basic healthcare delivery would be welcomed. Digital Health through tele-medicine and now AI (through remote triaging/screening and virtual health assistants) can fill in the void efficiently and effectively. This is why in less resourced countries there is more willingness to accept AI (see below figure).

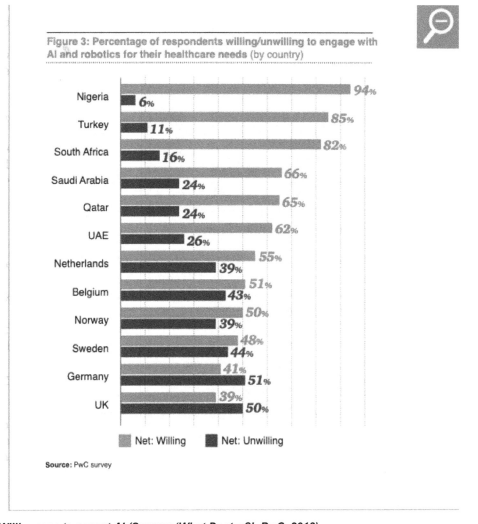

Figure 3: Percentage of respondents willing/unwilling to engage with AI and robotics for their healthcare needs (by country)

*Willingness to accept AI (Source: 'What Doctor?'- PwC, 2018)*

Yet, AI is not just applicable to low-resource settings or for substituting medical workforce, it is also useful to contain burgeoning costs that health services face irrespective of the country where they are located. While it is beyond the scope of this article to explain the reasons for the increasing costs, but to summarise quickly they are an ageing population, the chronic disease burden, inefficient health funding mechanisms and recurrent costs (read workforce salaries). AI can play a huge role in addressing most of these cost-drivers. Many countries and companies see the opportunity to do this. Hence, a growing interest and investment in AI in Healthcare from commercial enterprises (see below figure).

Funding activity for AI + healthcare companies, 2013 - 2017

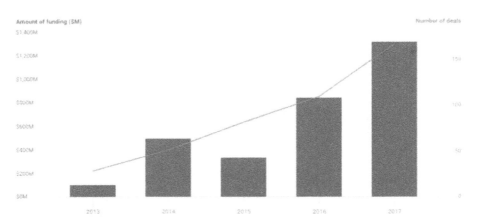

*Funding Activity for AI in Healthcare (Source: CB insights, 2018)*

This investment and interest will see more and more AI applications introduced into the healthcare market and service delivery in years to come. By informing new care models that are more efficient and effective, AI will not only contain costs of medical treatment but will also improve access and patient outcomes. How? Where there is repetitive and less complex medical activity, machine learning can simulate these functions for much lesser costs on the long run. This leaves human clinicians to drive and manage complex medical activity and spend time with patients more effectively. Also, low-cost AI technology delivered through economies of scale means wider availability of health services. A case in point is AI driven primary screening and virtual health assistants that are now increasingly being offered by several providers. Further, incorporation of machine learning in drug development can not only reduce the costs of development for the company but also decrease the price of medication when offered. In addition, AI driven diagnostics in laboratories and medical imaging departments can accelerate the diagnostic process and lessen the time spent in hospitals for patients, thus reducing costs and the risks associated with lengthy hospital stay.

These are just some of the examples, how AI can reduce costs and improve health outcomes. There will be as AI technology develops and gets used in healthcare, more examples to be seen. Therefore, AI will have its greatest impact in healthcare.

# Chapter 2: Why healthcare systems should adopt AI?

Keeping aside the buzz and hype about the utilization of AI in various disciplines and what mistakenly many assume it can accomplish, there are real merits in governments and decision-makers setting out strategies for adoption of AI in health service delivery. In this chapter, I will review the economic benefits of the application.

Of those health systems analyzed by the Commonwealth Fund in their performance rankings, people in the United States (US) and Australia had the highest out-of-pocket costs when accessing healthcare. This issue has arisen not for the lack of investment in healthcare by governments in these countries. In 2016, healthcare spending in the US increased by 4.3% to attain a figure of US$3.3 trillion or about US$10,348 per person. Of the US$3.3 trillion, US$1.1 trillion was spent on hospital care, US$92 billion on allied health services and about US$162.5 billion on nursing care facilities and retirement communities. Together these expenditures constituted approximately 45% of the 2016 health spend. Of the total health expenditure, individuals/household's contribution matched the government expenditure (28% of the total health expenditure). In Australia in 2015-16, the entire healthcare spend was AU$170.4 billion (an AU$6 billion increase compared to 2014-15). Of this, the government expenditure on public hospital services was AU$46.9 billion ,and on primary healthcare AU$34.6 billion. Expenditure by individuals accounted for 52.7% of non-government expenditure or 17.3% of total health expenditure. While governments continue to increase spending, this hasn't really made a serious dent on out-of-pocket costs.

One of the critical components of annual healthcare spending and pertinent to this article is the recurrent healthcare expenditure. Recurrent healthcare expenditure does not involve the acquisition of fixed assets and expenditure on capital but largely expenditure on wages, salaries and supplements. In Australia, recurrent healthcare expenditure constitutes a whopping 94% of the total health spending and in the US, about US$664.9 billion was spent on physician and clinical wages in 2016. Considering it is unlikely for wages to go down; it is hard to imagine recurrent healthcare expenditure decreasing and consequently, total healthcare spend decreasing.

AI technology, which has been around for decades but has only recently received widespread attention, is increasingly being applied in various aspects of healthcare (primarily in the US). While **AI is unlikely to replace human clinicians totally** (see chapter 14), many hospitals are using AI technology **to leverage their consultant's expertise** and in some cases **the AI applications are outperforming them**. I won't discuss the technologies and application in this chapter ( as it is covered in subsequent chapters) but I will discuss the costs of development of these technologies from a healthcare point of view.

*Healthcare costs are rising*

With traditional software development, the usual phases include discovery and analysis phase, prototype implementation and evaluation phase, minimum viable product and followed by product release. The costs associated with these phases, depending on the project sizes and complexity of the software, can constitute anywhere from US$10,000 to US$100,000[1]. However, development of AI programs (here I will consider Machine Learning based programs , not robotic applications, which adopt a different development model and consequently different cost models) have distinctive features to be considered in their development.

These aspects include the acquisition of large data sets to train the system and fine-tuning the algorithms that analyse the data. Where significant data sets cannot be obtained, data augmentation can be considered. Costs will be incurred in acquiring the data sets if not available in prior. However, in the context of healthcare government agencies and hospitals can provide this data for developers at no costs (if the AI program is being developed/customized for their exclusive use). So, the most cost impacting factor is whether the data is structured or not. Data doesn't have to be structured, there are several machine learning algorithms that are trained to analyse unstructured data. However, developing programs to review unstructured data incurs more costs. Even when structured data is available, there are processes like data cleansing and data type conversion, which add to the costs. The next

---

[1] This estimation does not take into consideration deployment, insurance and marketing costs.

distinctive feature is fine-tuning/customizing the machine learning algorithm to suit organization's requirements. As the healthcare context requires the program to have a high degree of accuracy (less false negatives and high true positive identification epidemiological speaking), many rounds of refinements of the algorithm will be required.

Even considering these distinctive features, which will add to the baseline costs ranging from US$50,000 to US$300,000; [2] you are looking at a range of total costs of US$60,000 to US$500,000 (depending on the organisation requirements and complexity of the AI software). If we consider in the US about US$664 billion (2016) and in Australia that AU$64 billion (2015-2016) was spent on hospital recurrent expenditure alone, a mere 0.016% allocation of the spend on developing AI technologies could fund development of at least 18 (hospital focused advanced machine learning based) applications per annum. The return of investment is not just economic but also improvement in patient outcomes because of avoidance of medical errors, improved medical/laboratory/radiological diagnosis and predictability of chronic disease outcomes. Considering the rapid advances machine learning based program have made in medical prediction, diagnosis and prognosis^ , governments and healthcare organizations should seriously consider focus on supporting the development and deployment of AI technologies not only for the serious dent these applications can make on recurrent health expenditure but also how they can significantly improve patient access.

---

[2] This estimation does not take into consideration deployment, insurance and marketing costs.

# The Technique

# Chapter 3: AI Techniques in Health

For those who are technophiles, what I discuss in this chapter is quite basic but for many with a health background, it may be the first time they are learning about these terms.

Let us start by defining Artificial Intelligence. I don't necessarily like the term 'Artificial Intelligence'. This term derives from the incorrect assumption intelligence has been primarily a biological construct so far and any intelligence that is now being derived outside the biological domain is artificial. In other words, intelligence is framed exclusively in reference to biologically derived intelligence. However, intelligence is a profound entity of its own with defined characteristics such as learning and reasoning. Human intelligence is not the most intelligence can be and as trends go, computing programs with their increasingly advanced algorithms can potentially in the next decade or so exceed the learning and reasoning powers of humans in some respects. Therefore, a source-based terminology for intelligence would be more appropriate to frame intelligence. In other words, computational intelligence would be more appropriate than artificial intelligence. There are no natural or artificial aspects to it. A better way of describing Artificial Intelligence would be 'Computational Intelligence' attributing the source of intelligence. However, to make it easy for us , I use in this book the commonly used term Artificial Intelligence (AI). While there are different ways of defining AI, I use a simple definition "***Human Intelligence established by machines***". This definition, obviously, does not cover all the nuances of what AI is or can do but gives you an indication of what AI is.

AI has been around since the 1960s. How come we had not heard of it as much as we do now? Two reasons: the emergence of cheap 'Graphical Processing Units (GPUs)' and an increase in 'Big Data'. So, what is a GPU? It is a processor designed to handle graphics operations. GPUs render graphics better than Central Processing Units (CPUs). GPUs now have become ubiquitous and cheap. The other reason for rise of AI is emergence of Big Data. Big Data is high volume complex data, which requires computational analysis. In the medical domain, Big Data can refer to medical images, bioinformatics data, patient records and administrative data. AI needs data to perform well and Big Data needs the power of AI for analysis. So, they have worked well hand in hand to lead to the rise of AI.

Now let us look at the types of AI. There are mainly two kinds: General AI and Narrow AI. General AI is when there is complete mirroring of human cognition including emotions. However, at this stage no one has been able to achieve that and is purely in the realm of science fiction. Though, narrow AI is now widely seen. Narrow AI is where computers can perform specific tasks as well as humans and sometimes-even better.

The most commonly used AI technique is 'Machine Learning'. So, what is Machine Learning? Machine Learning is about creating an algorithm that uses data to learn complex relationships or patterns in order to make accurate decisions. Rather than coding specific instructions to accomplish the task, you train the algorithm with large amounts of data so it can learn how to perform the task itself. The data tells the machine learning algorithm what the 'good' answer is. There are two categories of Machine Learning: Unsupervised Learning and Supervised Learning. Supervised learning is where data is labelled to train the algorithms and in unsupervised learning is where data is not labelled. The two categories have further subcategories, but I will not be covering them in this chapter.

However, I do want to discuss an advanced type of machine learning. Deep Learning or Deep Neural Network is based on creating layers of processing units or neurons with interconnections. These connections are weighted so they can be manipulated to arrive at relevant answers. The most common approach used in Deep Learning is Backpropagation, where information present in one layer informs the next layer. Once the algorithm is trained and deep learning is set in motion, it runs largely autonomous with little guidance. Also, it undergoes continuous improvement using the data fed into it.

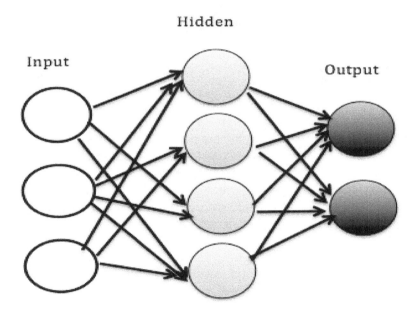

*Deep Learning Architecture*

The other forms of AI currently being used in healthcare are machine learning, natural language processing, expert systems, computer vision and robots. Natural Language Processing (NLP) is a set of technologies for human-like-processing of any natural language, oral or written, and includes both the interpretation and production of text, speech, dialogue etc. NLP techniques include symbolic, statistical and connectionist approaches and have been applied to machine translation, speech recognition, cross-language information retrieval, human-computer interactions and so forth. Some of these technologies, and certainly the effects, we see in normal societal IT products such as through email scanning for advertisements or auto-entry text for searches.

" Expert systems" is another established field of AI, in which the aim is to design systems that carry out significant tasks at the level of a human expert. Expert systems do not yet demonstrate general-purpose intelligence, but they have demonstrated equal and sometimes better reasoning and decision making in narrow domains compared to humans while conducting these tasks similar to how a human would do so. To achieve this function, an expert system can be provided with a computer representation of knowledge about a particular topic and apply this to give advice to human users. This concept was pioneered in medicine the 1980s by MYCIN, a system used to diagnose infections and INTERNIST an early diagnosis package. Recent knowledge-based expert systems combine more versatile and more rigorous engineering methods. These applications typically take a long time to develop and tend to have a narrow domain of expertise, although they are rapidly expanding. Outside of healthcare, these types of systems are often used for many other functions, such as trading stocks.

Another area is Computer Vision systems, which capture images (still or moving) from a camera and transforms or extract meanings from them to support understanding and interpretation. Replicating the power of human vision in a computer program is no easy task, but it attempts to do so by relying on a combination of mathematical methods, massive computing power to process real-world images and physical sensors. While great advances have been made with Computer Vision in such applications as face recognition, scene analysis, medical imaging and industrial inspection the ability to replicate the versatility of human visual processing remains elusive.

The final technique we cover here are Robots, which have been defined as "physical agents that perform tasks by manipulating the physical world" for which they need a combination of sensors (to perceive the environment) and effectors (to achieve physical effects in the environment). Many organisations have had increasing success in limited Robots which can be fixed or mobile. Mobile "autonomous" robots that use machine learning to extract sensor and motion models from data and which can make decisions on their own without relying on an operator are most relevant to this commentary, of which "self-driving" cars are well-known examples.

# Chapter 4: Why is Support Vector Machine popular in Medical AI?

Support Vector Machine (SVM) is becoming a popular machine learning algorithm to use when it comes to predictive analytics and diagnosis in medicine. While in non-medical disciplines, artificial neural networks have overtaken SVM's in popularity, SVMs continue to be widely used in machine learning driven medical data analysis. What is the reason for SVM's popularity in medicine? SVM models compared to neural networks are easier to explain, can work on small datasets , and in certain cases have comparable levels of accuracy.

 SVM is a supervised machine learning algorithm, which can be used both for classification and regression purposes. The current version of SVM was developed by Vladimir Vapnik and Corrina Cortes in the early 1990s. SVM works differentiating data items (support vectors) into two classes through a hyperplane (separating line) as illustrated in the below diagram. The further away the data items from the hyperplane the more confident one can be about the accuracy of the classification. The versatility of SVM is that it can be used for non-linear classification and even unsupervised machine learning classification (when data is unlabelled). In addition to classification, SVM can be used to build regression models i.e. prediction of outcomes based on medical data analysis.

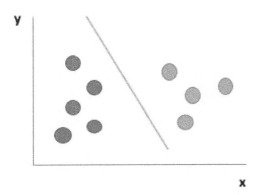

*Support Vector Machine Hyperplane*

Because of the simpleness of the algorithm and its ease in being able to analyse data it has been used in a wide variety of medical scenarios successfully including prediction of medication adherence in heart failure patients, predicting factors affecting preterm delivery, diagnosis of cancer conditions, prediction of development of dementia and diagnosis of schizophrenia. SVM has also been used to classify medical images. SVMs have noted to be having great accuracy and can work on small (but clean) datasets. However, they aren't suited for large datasets and unstructured datasets with overlapping classes.

# Chapter 5: Causal inference and hybrid approaches in Medical AI

Some time ago a twitter war (OK, maybe a vigorous debate) erupted between proponents of deep learning models and long-standing critics of deep learning approaches in AI. After following the conversation and my own study of the maths of probabilistic deep learning approaches, I have been thinking about alternative approaches to current Bayesian/back-propagation based deep learning models.

The versatility and deep impact (pun intended) of neural network models in pattern recognition, including in medicine, is well documented. Yet, the statistical approach/maths of deep learning is largely based on probability inference/Bayesian approaches. The neural networks of deep learning remember classes of relevant data and recognise to classify the same or similar data the next time around. It is kind of what we term 'generalisation' in research lingo, albeit for certain contexts only. Deep learning approaches have received acclaim because they are able to better capture invariant properties of the data and thus achieve higher accuracies compared to their shallow cousins (read supervised machine learning algorithms). As a high-level summary, deep learning algorithms adopt a non-linear and distributed representation approach to yield parametric models that can perform sequential operations on data that is fed into it. This ability has had profound implications in pattern recognition leading to various applications such as voice assistants, driver-less cars, facial recognition technology and image interpretation not to mention the development of the incredible AlphaGo, which has now evolved into AlphaGo zero. The potential of application of deep learning in medicine, where big data abounds, is vast. Some recent medical applications include EHR data mining and analysis, medical imaging interpretation (the most popular one being diabetic retinopathy diagnosis), and non-knowledge based clinical decision support systems. Better yet, the realisation of this potential is just beginning as newer forms of deep learning algorithms are developed in the various Big-Tech and academic labs. Then what is the issue?

Aside from the often cited 'interpretability/black-box' issue associated with neural networks and it's limitations in dealing with hierarchal structures and global generalisation, there is the 'elephant in the room' i.e. no inherent representation of causality. In medical diagnosis, the probability is important, but causality is more so. In fact, the whole science of medical treatment is based on causality. You don't want to use doxycycline instead of doxorubicin to treat Hodgkin's Lymphoma or the vice versa for Lyme Disease. How do you know if the underlying is Hodgkin's Lymphoma or Lyme Disease? The diagnosis is based on a combination of objective clinical examination, physical findings, sero-pathological tests, medical imaging. All premised on a causation sequence i.e. Borrelia leads to Lyme Disease and EB virus/family history leads to Hodgkin's. This is why we adopt Randomised Control Trials, even with its inherent faults, as the gold standard for the incorporation of evidence-based treatment approaches. If an understanding of causal mechanisms is the basis of clinical medicine and practice, then there are only so much deep learning approaches can do for medicine. This is why I believe there needs to be a serious conversation amongst AI academics and the developer community about the adoption of 'causal discovery algorithms' or better yet 'hybrid approaches ( a combination of probabilistic and causal discovery approaches)'.

We now have algorithms that search for causal structure information from data. They are represented by causal graphical models as illustrated below:

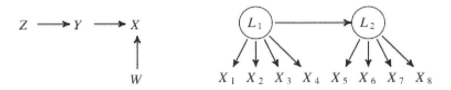

*Acyclic Graph Models (Source: Malinsky and Danks, 2017[3])*

While the causal search models do not provide you with a comprehensive causal list, they provide enough information for you to infer a diagnosis and treatment approach (in medicine). There have been numerous successes documented with this approach and different causal search algorithms developed over the past many decades. Professor Judea Pearl, one of the godfathers of causal inference approaches and an early proponent of AI has outlined structural causal models, a coherent mathematical basis for the analysis of causes and counterfactuals. You can read an introduction version here:
https://www.ncbi.nlm.nih.gov/pmc/articles/PMC2836213/

I think it is probably a time now to pause and think, especially in the context of medicine, if a causal approach is better in some contexts than a deep learning gradient informed approach. Even better if we can think of a syncretic approach. Believe me, I am an avid proponent of the application of deep learning in medicine/healthcare. There are some contexts, where back-propagation is better than hypothetico-deductive inference especially when terabytes/petabytes of unstructured data accumulates in the healthcare system. Also, there are limitations to causal approaches. Sometimes probabilistic approaches are not that bad as outlined by critics.

---

[3] D. Malinsky and D. Danks (2018) "Causal Discovery Algorithms: A Practical Guide," *Philosophy Compass* 13: e12470.

However, close-mindedness to an alternative approach to probabilistic deep learning models and total reliance on this approach is a sure-bet to failure of realisation of the full potential of AI in Medicine and even worse failure of the full adoption of AI in Medicine. To address this some critics of prevalent deep learning approaches are advocating for a Hybrid approach, whereby a combination of deep learning and causal approaches are utilised. I strongly believe there is merit in this recommendation, especially in the context of the application of AI in medicine/healthcare.

A development in this direction is the 'Causal Generative Neural Network'. This framework is trained using back-propagation but unlike previous approaches, capitalises on both conditional independences and distributional asymmetries to identify bivariate and multivariate causal structures. The model not only estimates a causal structure but also a differential generative model of the data. I will be most certainly following the developments with this framework and more generally hybrid approaches especially in the context of its application in medicine, but I think all those interested in the application of AI in Medicine should be having a conversation about this matter.

# The Application

# Chapter 6: Combining Image Analysis and Natural Language Processing to deliver precision medicine

As medical care evolves, clinicians and researchers are exploring the use of technology to improve the quality and effectiveness of medical care. In this regard, technology is being used to deliver precision medicine. This form of medicine is a new approach that focuses on using genomic, environmental and personal data to customize and deliver precise form of medical treatment. Hence the name 'precision medicine'. One of the most influential factors, in recent years, in delivering precision medicine has been AI. In specific one of its forms Machine Learning (ML). ML, which uses computation to analyse and interpret various forms of medical data to identify patterns and predict outcomes has shown increasing success in various areas of healthcare delivery. In this article, I discuss how computer vision and natural language processing, which use ML can be used to deliver precision medicine. I also discuss the technical and ethical challenges associated with the approaches and what the future holds if the challenges are addressed.

## Image Analysis

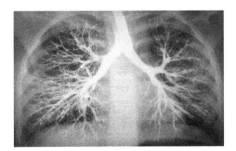

Various forms of medical imaging techniques like X-rays, CT, MRI and Nuclear imaging techniques are being used by clinicians to assist their diagnosis and treatment of various conditions ranging from cancers to simple fractures. The importance of these techniques in devising specific treatments has become critical in recent years. However, the dependency on a limited subset of trained medical specialists (Radiologists) to interpret and confirm the images has meant in many instances increase with the diagnosis and treatment times. The task of classifying and segmenting medical images can not only be tedious but take a lot of time. Computer Vision (CV), a form of AI that enables computers to interpret images and relate what the images are, has in the recent years shown a lot of promise and success. CV is now being applied in medicine to interpret radiological, fundoscopic and histopathological images. The most publicized success of recent years has been the interpretation of retinopathy images to diagnose diabetic and hypertensive retinopathy. The use of CV, powered by neural networks (an advanced form of ML), is said to take over the tedious task of segmenting and classifying medical images and enable preliminary or differential diagnosis. This approach is stated not only to accelerate the process of diagnosis and treatment but also provide more time for the radiologists to focus on complex imaging interpretations.

**Natural Language Processing**

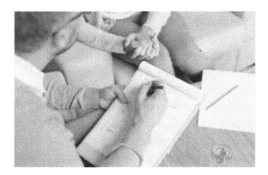

As with CV, Natural Language Processing (NLP) has had a great impact on society in the form of voice assistants, spam filters, and chat-bots. NLP applications are also being used in healthcare in the form of virtual health assistants and in recent years have been identified to have potential in analysing clinical notes and spoken instructions from clinicians. This ability of NLP can lessen the burden for busy clinicians who are encumbered by a need to document all their patient care in electronic health records (EHRs). By freeing up the time in writing copious notes, NLP applications can enable clinicians to focus more of their time with patients. In the recent period NLP techniques have been used to analyse even unstructured (free form and written notes) data, which makes it useful in instances where written data is not available in the digital form or there are non-textual data. By integrating NLP applications in EHRs, the workflow and delivery of healthcare can be accelerated.

**Combination of Approaches**

Precision medicine is premised on customization of medical care based on individual profile of patients. By combining NLP and CV techniques, the ability to deliver precision medicine s greatly increased. For example, NLP techniques can scroll through past medical notes to identify previously diagnosed conditions and medical treatment and present the information in a summary to doctors even as the patient presents to the clinic or to the emergency department. Once in the clinic or emergency department, NLP voice recognition applications can analyse conversation between the patient and clinicians and document it in the form of patient notes for the doctor to review and confirm. This process can free up time for the doctor and ensure accuracy of notes. As the doctor identifies the condition affecting the patient and relies on confirmation through relevant medical imaging, automated or semi-automated CV techniques can accelerate the confirmation process. Thus, a cohesive process that can accelerate the time in which the patient receives necessary medical treatment.

Let us see how this works in a fictitious example. Mr Carlyle, an avid cyclist, meets with an accident on his way to work when an automobile swerves into the bike lane and flings him from his bicycle. The automobile driver calls in an ambulance when he notices Mr Carlyle seated and grimacing with pain. The ambulance after arrival having entered his unique patient identifier number, which is accessed from his smartwatch, rushes him to the nearest emergency department. The AI agent embedded in the hospital's patient information system identifies Mr Carlyle through his patient identifier number and pulls out his medical details including his drug allergies. This information is available for the clinicians in the emergency department to review even as Mr Carlyle arrives. After being placed in an emergency department bay, the treating doctor uses an NLP application to record, analyse and document the conversation between her and Mr Carlyle. This option allows the doctor to focus most of her time on Mr Carlyle. The doctor suspects a fracture of the clavicle and has Mr Carlyle undergo an X-ray. The CV application embedded in the imaging information system has detected a mid-shaft clavicular fracture and relays the diagnosis back to the doctor. The doctor, prompted by an AI clinical decision support application embedded in the patient information system, recommends immobilization and a sling treatment for Mr Carlyle along with pain killers. His pain killer excludes NSAIDs as the AI agent has identified he is allergic to aspirin.

## Challenges

The above scenario while presenting a clear example of how AI, in specific CV and NLP applications, can be harnessed to deliver prompt and personalized medical care is yet contingent on the technologies to deliver such outcomes. Currently, CV techniques have not achieved the confidence of regulatory authorities nor clinicians to allow automated medical imaging diagnosis (except in minor instances such as diabetic retinopathy interpretation) and neither are NLP applications embedded in EHRs to allow automatic recording, analysis and recording of patient conversations. While some applications have been released in the market to analyse unstructured data, external validation and wide acceptance of these type of applications are some years away. Coupled with this technical and regulatory challenges is the ethical challenges of enabling autonomy of non-human agents to guide and deliver clinical care. Further issues may arise due to the use of patient identifiers to extract historical details even if it is for medical treatment if the patient hasn't consented so. Yet, the challenges can be overcome as AI technology improves and governance structures to protect patient privacy, confidentiality and safety are established. As focus on the ethics of application of AI in healthcare increases and technological limitations of AI application get resolved, the fictitious scenario may become a reality not too far into the future.

## Conclusion

There is a natural alignment between AI and precision medicine as the power of AI methods such as NLP and CV can be leveraged to analyse bio-metric data and deliver personalize medical treatment for patients. With appropriate safeguards, the use of AI in delivering precision medicine can only benefit both the patient and clinician community. One can based on the rapidly evolving AI technology predict the coming years will see wider adaption of precision care models in medicine and thus AI techniques.

# Chapter 7: Tackling the global chronic disease burden through AI

The World Health Organisation estimates major chronic diseases account for almost 60 percent of mortality and 43 percent of the global burden of disease. In the US, half of the population has some form of chronic diseases. However; responses to date to address the chronic disease have been largely inadequate. The main reasons for this include a non-evidenced based approach to managing the burden, incorrect beliefs about the cause and distribution of chronic diseases, system and financial constraints. Evidence suggests that when chronic disease patients receive effective treatments, self-management support, and regular follow-up better health outcomes ensue.

*Chronic disease management is complex*

Given that the current and entrenched acute care-oriented health systems appear to be struggling to reorient to preventative and primary care approaches; new and innovative models for chronic disease care are being welcomed by healthcare professionals. One such novel approach is the use of AI in the treatment of chronic diseases. AI has been found to enable new evidence-based approaches to treat chronic diseases, reduce costs and enable better patient compliance with treatment. AI is increasingly being employed in medicine with promising results and it's use in addressing chronic disease burden will similarly have a profound effect.

With the availability of health data from several sources including smartphones, wearable devices, electronic health records and other sources, there lies an opportunity to analyse this data to formulate appropriate and personalised treatment and disease management regimens. Previously, the lack of appropriate tools and infrastructure to undertake analysis has meant much of health data lay unused. With the advent of machine learning and associated computing infrastructure, there is an ability to harness and analyse patient data to deliver personalised healthcare. This opportunity matters as we observe ever-increasing avoidable hospitalisations and readmissions.

Use of machine learning can help in identifying at-risk patients and enable targeted intervention to prevent hospitalisations and readmissions. This approach not only can improve patient outcomes but can also save costs. It is estimated by the US *Agency for Healthcare Research and Quality* over $30 billion is spent on hospitalisations in the US, of which over 50 % is due to chronic diseases. By reducing hospitalisations through intensive treatment of identified patients in outpatient settings and preventing readmissions through early intervention and better care, billions of dollars can be saved.

Of all the chronic conditions, Cardiovascular Disease is one of the most costly and prevalent chronic conditions in the US and stands amongst the top 10 costliest and prevalent chronic diseases in the world. I now highlight how AI is assisting the treatment and management of this condition.

Cardiovascular Diseases involves the heart and blood vessels and includes conditions such as coronary heart disease and heart failure. By far the leading cause of death across the world are cardiovascular diseases. Therefore, early prediction and diagnoses of heart conditions can prevent unnecessary deaths. In recent years, machine learning algorithms have shown great promise in predicting the risk of heart attacks and strokes. Currently, primary care clinicians use risk calculators to assess patient's risk of developing heart diseases. However, these tools rely on data captured at that moment and do not assess longitudinal data. However, machine learning algorithms through a combination of data mining and analysing electronic health records can automatically predict the risk of heart diseases. In fact, a study from the Francis Crick Institute demonstrated an AI model that could beat doctors in predicting heart disease deaths. The model trained on electronic health data of over 80,000 patients in the UK searches for patterns by picking the most relevant variables to predict the risk of heart diseases.

Machine learning algorithms can also be used to analyse electrocardiograms (ECGs) and echocardiograms to detect heart diseases such as ventricular dysfunction in its early stages. Early detection can help with better management of the condition. Here the model, similar to the heart disease predictor model, is trained on a large database of ECG and echocardiogram data to recognise a specific type of heart diseases. Then after it is tested on an independent set of patient data to assess accuracy, sensitivity and specificity. Machine learning algorithms such as convolutional neural networks can be used to analyse echocardiography and MRI cardiac images to recognise abnormalities thus improving clinical work flow and enabling cost savings. Finally, with the aid of wearable devices and smart watches, AI tools can help in identifying early warning signs of heart attacks. Devices that use ECG sensors can detect abnormal heart rate and rhythms but in conjunction with machine learning algorithms can monitor the heart rate and rhythm to track efficacy of cardiac interventions and lifestyle changes.

The above was only one of the chronic conditions where AI has shown usefulness, AI has also shown efficacy in managing diabetes (see next chapter), detecting cancer conditions, helping with treatment of chronic respiratory conditions and improving mental well-being of mental health patients. Thus, AI as a technology has promising application in the area of chronic disease treatment and management. Collaboration between academic centres, AI vendors and health services will be required to progress the use of AI to address the chronic disease burden.

# Chapter 8: Managing Diabetes through AI

The World Health Organisation estimates major chronic diseases account for almost 60 per cent of mortality and 43 per cent of the global burden of disease. However; responses to date to this alarming issue have been mostly inadequate. The main reasons for this include a non-evidenced based approach to managing the burden, incorrect beliefs about the cause and distribution of chronic diseases, system and financial constraints. Evidence suggests that when chronic disease patients receive effective treatments, self-management support, and regular follow-up better health outcomes ensue. Given that the current and entrenched acute care-oriented health systems appear to be struggling to reorient to preventative and primary care approaches; new and innovative models for chronic disease care are being welcomed by healthcare professionals. One such novel approach is the use of Artificial Intelligence (AI) techniques like machine learning in the treatment of chronic diseases. AI has been found to enable new evidence-based approaches to treat chronic diseases, reduce costs and enable better patient compliance with treatment.

The Australian Government describes chronic diseases as a range of complex long-lasting health conditions. The Centers for Disease Control in the USA includes heart disease, stroke, cancer, type 2 diabetes, obesity, and arthritis as chronic diseases. Common to all these conditions are pre-existing risk factors, whether it be modifiable or absolute or both. For conditions such as type 2 diabetes and heart diseases, health behaviours such as physical activity and diet/nutrition are critical modifiable risk factors. Targeting these behaviours has been found to be very useful in preventing or delaying the emergence of type 2 diabetes and heart diseases. Also, it has been found a frequent interaction between physicians and patients support medication/treatment adherence, increase in physical activity and proper nutrition.

While governments and health services have an obligation to deliver quality healthcare for all patients including chronic disease patients, they have generally failed with this objective. It is known prevention is better than cure in the context of chronic diseases treatment. It is also known preventing or delaying the emergence of diabetes type 2 and heart diseases can not only be beneficial for individuals but also financially beneficial for health systems. AI enabled applications have a significant role in realizing these benefits. The most efficient approach to realise these benefits is by using AI techniques like machine learning to modify risk behaviours and predict the development of chronic conditions.

Both for pre-diabetic and diabetic patients, it is known modification of risk factors like overweightness, poor nutrition and sedentary lifestyle mitigates the progression of diabetes mellitus type 2. By using machine learning and natural language processing techniques, health services and clinicians can be connected to patients between their visits, monitor their health parameters and coach them towards a healthy lifestyle.

*Proper nutrition is important to control blood glucose levels in Diabetic patients*

Evidence indicates frequent communication between physician's patients with cardiovascular risk factors coupled with monitoring of patient-derived data like blood sugar levels, physical activity levels, dietary intake and medication use, limit the progression of the disease. Also, it has been found a frequent interaction between physicians and patients supports regular visits. When health services are stretched with their resources and cannot afford to provide constant human engagement with their diabetic patients, AI enabled applications offered through mobile platforms can fill in this void and support compliance with treatment and regular visits to the clinics for follow-up management.

The other reasons health services should consider employing AI techniques with regards to diabetic or pre-diabetic patients are:
a) evidence from prior studies that AI enabled applications improve compliance with treatment and encourage regular visits to clinics.
b) ability to integrate with electronic health records of the patient and analyse laboratory results and other biological parameters of pre-diabetic patients to predict their risk of developing diabetes.
c) Through the use of computer vision and machine learning, diabetic retinopathy can be detected even without an optometrist or ophthalmologist. This feature is very useful in resource-poor settings where specialist workforce may not be available on site to interpret retinal fundoscopic images.

*Regular blood glucose checks are necessary for Diabetic patients*

By integrating AI applications with electronic health records and offering AI enabled virtual health coaching for at-risk patients, health services and governments not only can mitigate the development of advanced disease in patients but also reduce the costs involved in treating and managing these conditions. Also, AI enabled applications can replace some of the costly human-led interventions with more sustainable solutions thus saving health services recurrent costs.

# Chapter 9: Chatbots in Provision of Healthcare

Access to healthcare/medical services has hidden and overt barriers including distance, costs and resource constraints. Health services have been pursuing various options to address these barriers. Provision of healthcare from a distance or remotely can address some of these barriers. The emergence of chatbots, smart algorithms that can engage in conversation with humans, has presented an opportunity to deliver healthcare advice or counselling remotely at lower costs. We are now seeing increasing use of chatbots in healthcare to improve access to healthcare. Healthcare chatbots can engage in one-on-one conversations with patients through an automated process reducing the role of human involvement in the provision of healthcare while vastly improving access for patients to qualified health advice.

Healthcare chatbots not only can improve access but can also help with medication management, schedule medical appointments and intervene in emergency medical situations. Through the provision of chatbots, health services can connect patients with clinicians and allied health staff remotely. Also, chatbots can provide customised nutritional, rehabilitation and mental health counselling by tapping into medical databases. Chatbots are also being used to screen non-emergency patients so as not to overload busy emergency departments or hospitals, thus helping in reducing costs for both health services and patients. Further, chatbots are being used for billing, inventory and insurance claims management.

With advances in Natural Language Processing, chatbots are no longer restricted to text-based conversations but also can engage in voice-based conversations with humans. This type of conversation is especially useful for older patient groups, who are not comfortable typing instructions/information. Also, voice-based conversation can be useful to provide companionship to aged individuals. Because of the versatility of the uses of chatbots, we will continue to see an expanding role of chatbots in the healthcare sector.

While it is appealing to think medical chatbots will replace human clinicians in some areas altogether, the fact is medical chatbots can provide advice, not a diagnosis. Medical chatbots work well in screening medical conditions and referring serious or relevant patients to healthcare services for medical care. By providing automated 24/7 screening and referral service without dependency on the human workforce, costs are reduced for health services. For patients, there is improved access to qualified medical or healthcare advice. However, chatbots offered through smartphones or other digital devices cannot replace the medical environment and equipment that serious medical conditions require. Even with advances in chatbot technology, there will be a need for patients to attend an officially designated medical service where their care is supervised by human clinicians. So, healthcare/medical chatbots will complement human clinicians not replace them.

*Chatbots can assist with lifestyle and nutritional advice*

Prominent examples of healthcare chatbots are Babylon Health, Ada Health, Sensely and Buoy Health amongst many others. Babylon Health (https://www.babylonhealth.com) is a British start-up that offers online medical consultation through an AI-driven application. It asks patients to enter their medical details and offers differential diagnosis and referral services. It has tied up with the UK's National Health Service to screen patients in certain areas. Ada Health (https://ada.com) similarly is symptom checking chatbot that commenced in Europe and has now expanded to the United States. Like the Babylon app, it asks questions of patients and compares the answers to cases from its medical database to provide explanation and differential diagnosis. Sensely (http://www.sensely.com) is a virtual medical assistant that can assess patients' symptoms using speech, text, images and video. By having a virtual persona on the screen and offering a choice of text and speech to communicate it has an added appeal over the Babylon and Ada health applications. Buoy Health (https://www.buoyhealth.com) developed by Harvard Innovation Labs is also a symptom checker and its algorithm has been trained on medical data from over 18,000 medical papers, medical data from 5 million patients and approximately 1,700 conditions. All these apps increase access to medical care for patients and alleviate the burden on stretched medical services by undertaking preliminary screening of patients before referring genuine and serious patients. The apps also provide a safe and non-judgemental portal to ask medical questions. However, as discussed earlier caution must be adopted with the advice provided and it must be noted confirmatory diagnosis can be delivered by human clinicians only.

There are technological limitations relating to the algorithms inability to appropriately recognise and analyse the human conversational inputs but in case of medical chatbots, their inability to recognise signs and symptoms of certain medical conditions, which require visual and tactile examination are limitations. Also, the chatbots are reliant on databases and patient input to analyse information and provide advice. If there are limitations in the databases and in the information provided by the patient, inaccurate advice can be provided. So, it is important in the current period that vendors or healthcare services let users know their healthcare chatbots are providing preliminary advice and that final advice is to be confirmed by their respective healthcare service.

Advances in artificial intelligence will see addition of computer vision, virtual faces, deep learning and improved natural language processing abilities to healthcare chatbot functioning thus not only enhancing their capability to recognise and analyse human conversations better but also screen medical conditions and appeal to humans better. Also, chatbots will increasingly be used by stretched healthcare services and insurance organisations to screen their patient populations or clients so only genuine patients are referred to hospitals and primary care clinics. Further, doctors will recommend all their chronic condition patients, especially those who require nutritional, exercise and medical management advice, to download and use chatbot applications to help them manage their condition. In addition, chatbots will be increasingly used in hospital and health service lobbies to help patients navigate the building and services being offered.

# Chapter 10: The role of AI in addressing healthcare challenges in developing countries

In 2018, while making an opening speech at an Artificial Intelligence (AI) in Health conference in Dubai, I mentioned that AI techniques can be used to address some of the intractable health issues in developing countries. This comment was picked up by a journalist of an online news site and reported as the headline of a news item covering the conference. However, the journalist also mentioned I hadn't provided any details to qualify my comments. To my defence, the focus of my speech was not about this topic. Subsequently, in a conversation a week ago with the founder of an US-based AI health start-up, we discussed the multitude of opportunities in using AI enabled health services in developing countries and how few are aware of these opportunities. These circumstances have ed me to articulate the benefits of AI in health in the context of developing countries. Here, I use India as a typical developing country but many of the processes I discuss can potentially be used in other developing countries.

First, let us discuss some of the common issues that health services in developing countries face. A common grievance of health services is the lack of a qualified workforce to treat and manage patients. Where health services have qualified personnel, they are overloaded with patients affecting the quality of the service they provide. The other common issue is the urban-rural maldistribution of qualified physicians. The preference of physicians to practice in urban health centres has led to a skewed distribution favouring urban centres and disadvantaging rural communities. In spite of government initiatives to push quality rural health services, the urban-rural divide is to stay. Another prominent issue is the variability in the quality of health services provided in different parts of the country and sometimes within the same region or city. This inconsistency is because of poor monitoring of health services by national accreditation bodies or poor compliance with quality standards by health services. Further, outbreaks of infectious diseases because of mainly environmental reasons has become alarmingly frequent in developing countries. Poor surveillance infrastructure means these outbreaks can progress to epidemics in a span of days. These aren't the only health system concerns in developing countries but are areas that I think will benefit from the application of AI techniques.

India with its massive population of 1.35 billion (2018 population estimate) is in dire need of strong health infrastructure and government policy to service the nation's health needs. India, just like many developing countries, has significant challenges in delivering this requirement. A combination of an increasing burden from chronic diseases, a large ageing population, qualified personnel shortage, urban-rural divide, low government investment in health, inadequate health insurance coverage and variable quality of health service delivery have contributed to this state of affairs. However, the Government of India has been lately active in firming up the health policy and strengthening the health infrastructure. One of the major initiatives of the government was the release of the National Health Policy last year with an aim to reinvigorate the healthcare delivery in India by increasing health spending, establishing national quality standards, promoting evidence-based healthcare and introduction of digital health initiatives. With regards to the latter objective, the intention to set up a National Digital Health Authority and promote interoperable Electronic Health Record systems across India will create a strong foundation for digital health innovations to be applied. This digital platform will also provide opportunities for Foreign Direct Investment (FDI) and contribute to further growth of digital health in India. As digital health initiatives ramp up in India, opportunities for application of AI will also open up.

*Developing countries like India face qualified medical workforce shortages*

So how would AI applications help the Indian health system? Earlier, I discussed the healthcare delivery challenges developing countries face. The same difficulties apply to India too. AI systems driven by deep neural networks and computer vision have matched accuracy levels of human clinicians in interpreting radiological, fundoscopic and histopathological images. Intelligent agents are also being used to mine data and analyse electronic health records to assist clinicians in the medical diagnosis and predicting mortality of patients. Also, machine learning and natural language processing driven mobile applications are being used to communicate with patients and aid medication adherence, healthy lifestyles and schedule visits to doctors. Further, AI applications are being used in hospitals to predict the length of stay of patients and formulate treatment plans for them. All of these developments are detailed in several academic journals and the media. Application of these agents will have a profound effect on the Indian healthcare landscape, where a shortage of qualified specialists and diagnostic centres abound. While the AI systems may not be able to replicate all the capabilities of the medical specialists, it will in combination with telemedicine approaches be able to increase healthcare access for underserved communities and alleviate the burden of overstretched health services.

AI systems can also aid in the improvement of the quality of healthcare by reducing the variability of healthcare delivery and enabling evidence-based practice across the country. By incorporating government sanctioned and thoroughly evaluated AI applications in healthcare delivery, the standardisation of healthcare delivery can be achieved. With inconsistency in healthcare delivery and non-evidence-based practices being common in India, roll out of authorised clinical decision support systems that run through machine learning processes will contribute to standardisation of healthcare delivery. Also, AI systems through ongoing analysis of ecological, biogeographical and public health data can alert authorities about outbreaks of infectious diseases and help contain the spread. For example, in recent years machine learning has been used to identify sources of outbreaks. During the Ebola outbreak in Africa, machine learning was used to analyse ecological data to determine the bat species harbouring Ebola virus and contain the spread of the disease. Thus, AI agents can also be used to strengthen India's communicable disease surveillance infrastructure.

While the use of AI applications presents significant promise for the Indian healthcare system, one has also to be cognizant of the challenges in applying AI approaches. AI applications rely on a robust digital health foundation including ongoing access to electronic patient data and patient/population information management systems. With the Indian digital health infrastructure being nascent at best, the widespread roll-out of AI applications can be a challenge. Also, with the low number of qualified health informaticians, machine learning trained data scientists and AI focused entities in India, there may be increased reliance on overseas companies to support the roll-out of AI applications. There are also issues like bias, lack of contextual reasoning and explainability problems that accompany AI applications. However, with advances in AI technology, some these issues have now been addressed with a number of solutions available.

To harness the benefit of AI approaches, the Indian government has to formulate a definitive AI strategy. A strategy that amongst many other things outlines the regulatory framework and implementation strategy for the roll-out of AI in India. The immense benefits that come through the application of AI can be only be realised through the boldness and proactiveness of the Indian government. By pushing forward a national AI strategy and setting up an AI-enabled healthcare delivery system, India can be a leading example for other countries as to how critical healthcare challenges can be addressed through AI approaches.

# The Caution

# Chapter 11: Caution regarding AI (a medical perspective)

To borrow Professor Dan Ariely's quote about Big Data, AI is like teenage sex: everyone talks about it, nobody really knows how to do it, everyone thinks everyone else is doing it, so everyone claims they are doing it.

However, this may be a too harsh commentary about the state of AI affairs. Notwithstanding the overstatements about the capabilities AI by some; there is some substance behind the hype with the demonstrated benefits of deep learning, natural language processing and robotics in various aspects of our lives. In Medical Informatics, the area I can credibly comment, neural networks and data mining have been employed to enhance the ability of human clinicians to diagnose and predict medical conditions, and in some instances like medical imaging and histo-pathological diagnosis, AI applications have met or exceeded the accuracy of human clinicians. In terms of economics, AI deserves the attention it is getting. The top 100 AI companies have raised more than US$11.7 billion in revenue and even back in 2015, about 49 billion US$ revenue was generated just in the North American Market. Countries like China have invested massively in AI research and start-ups, with some forecasting the Chinese AI industry exceeding US$150 billion by 2030. In other instances, like the political sphere, AI has received high profile recognition with the appointment of the first AI Minister in the world in U.A.E.

However, one has to be aware of the limitations with AI and the amount of research and analysis that is yet to be undertaken for us to confidently accept a ubiquitous AI system our lives. I state this as a vocal proponent of application of AI techniques especially in Medicine (as my earlier articles and book chapter indicate) but also as one who is aware of the 'AI Winter' and 'IBM Watson/MD Anderson' episodes that have occurred in the past. Plus, there is the incident that happened yesterday where a driverless Uber car was responsible for a fatality in Arizona. So, in this article, I list from a healthcare perspective, three main limitations in terms of adoptability of AI technologies. This analysis is based on current circumstances, which considering the rapid developments that are occurring in AI research may not apply into the future.

## 1) Machine Learning Limitations
The three main limitations I see with machine learning are *Data-feed*, *Model Complexity* and *Computing Times*.

In machine learning the iterative aspect of learning is important. Good machine learning models rely on data preparation and ongoing availability of good data. If you don't have good data to train the machine learning model (in supervised learning) and there is no new data, the pattern recognition ability of the model is moot. For example, in the case of radiology, if the images being fed into the deep learning algorithms tend to come with underlying biases (like images from a particular ethnic group or images from a particular region) the diagnostic abilities and accuracy rates of the model would be limited. Also, reliance on historical data to train algorithms may not be particularly useful for forecasting novel instances of drug side-effects or treatment resistance. Further, cleaning up and capturing data that are necessary for these models to function will provide a logistical challenge. Think of the efforts required to digitize handwritten patient records.

With regards to model complexity, it will be pertinent to describe deep learning (a form of machine learning) here. Deep Learning ,in essence, is a mathematical model where software programs learn to classify patterns using neural networks. For this learning, one of the methods used is backpropagation or backprop that adjusts mathematical weights between nodes-so that an input leads to right outputs. By scaling up the layers and adding more data, deep learning algorithms are to solve complex problems. The idea is to match the cognition processes a human brain employs. However, in reality, pattern recognition alone can't resolve all problems, especially so all medical problems. For example, when a decision has to be made in consultation with the family to take off mechanical ventilation for a comatose patient with inoperable intra-cerebral haemorrhage. The decision making in this instance is beyond the capability of a deep learning-based program.

The third limitation with machine learning is the current capabilities of computational resources. With the current resources like GPU cycles and RAM configurations, there are limitations as to how much you can bring down the training errors to reasonable upper bounds. This means the limitation impacts the accuracy of model predictions. This has been particularly pertinent with medical prediction and diagnostic applications, where matching the accuracy of human clinicians in some medical fields has been challenging. However, with the emergence of quantum computing and predicted developments in this area, some of these limitations will be overcome.

### 2) Ethico-legal Challenges
The ethico-legal challenges can be summarized as 'Explainability', 'Responsibility' and 'Empathy'.

A particular anxiety about artificial intelligence is that decisions made by complex opaque algorithms cannot be explained even by the designers (the black box issue). This becomes critical in the medical field, where decisions either made directly or indirectly through artificial intelligence applications can impact on patient lives. If an intelligent agent responsible for monitoring a critical patient incorrectly interprets a medical event and administers a wrong drug dosage, it will be important for stakeholders to understand what led to the decision. However, if the underlying complexity of the neural network means the decision-making path cannot be understood; it does present a serious problem. The challenge in explaining opaque algorithms is termed as the *interpretability* problem. Therefore, it is important for explainable AI or transparent AI applications to be employed for medical purposes. The medical algorithm should be fully auditable when and where (real-time and after the fact) required. To ensure the acceptability of AI applications in the healthcare system, researchers /developers need to work on accountable and transparent mathematical structures when devising AI applications.

When a robotic radical prostatectomy goes wrong or when a small cell pulmonary tumour is missed in an automated radiology service, who becomes responsible for the error? The developer? The hospital? The regulatory authority(which approved the use of the device or program)? As AI applications get incorporated in medical decision making and interventions, regulatory and legal bodies need to work with AI providers to set up appropriate regulatory and legal frameworks to guide deployment and accountability. Also, a thorough process of evaluation of new AI medical applications, before they can be used in practice, will be required to be established especially if an autonomous operation is the goal. Further, authorities should work with clinical bodies to establish clinical guidelines/protocols to govern the application of AI programs in medical interventions.

*AI medical decision making should be interpretable*

One of the important facets of medical care is the patient-clinician interaction/interface. Even with current advances in Robotics and intelligent agent programming, the human empathetic capabilities far exceed that those of AI applications. AI is dependent on a statistically sound logic process that intends to minimise or eliminate errors. This can be termed by some as cold or cut-and-dry unlike the variable emotions and risk-taking approach humans employ. In medical care, clinicians need to adopt a certain level of connection and trust with the patients they are treating. It is hard to foresee in the near future, AI-driven applications/robots replacing humans in this aspect.

However, researchers are already working on classifying and coding emotions:
https://www2.ucsc.edu/dreams/Coding/emotions.html

Also, robots are being developed with eerily realistic facial expressions:
https://www.hansonrobotics.com/sophia/

So maybe the cynicism about AI's usefulness in this area is not all that deserved, I think?

### 3) Acceptability and Adoptability:
While I think the current technological limitations with machine learning and robotics can be addressed in the near future, it will be a harder challenge for AI providers to convince the general public to accept autonomous AI applications, especially those that make decisions impacting on their lives. AI to an extent is pervasive already with the availability of voice-driven personal assistants, chatbots, driverless cars, learning home devices, predictive streaming etc. There hasn't been a problem for us in accepting these applications in our lives. However, when you have AI agents replacing critical positions that were previously held by humans; it can be confronting especially so in medical care. There is thus a challenge for AI developers and companies to ease the anxiousness of public in accepting autonomous AI systems. Here, I think, pushing explainable or transparent applications can make it easier for the public to accept AI agents.

The other challenge, from a medical perspective, is the adoption of AI applications by clinicians and healthcare organizations. I don't think the concern for clinicians is that AI agents will replace them but the issues are rather the limited understanding clinicians have about AI techniques (what goes behind the development), apprehensiveness about the accuracy of these applications especially in a litigious environment and scepticism as to whether the technologies can alleviate clinician's stretched schedules. For healthcare organizations, the concerns are whether there are cost efficiencies and cost-benefits with investment into AI technologies, whether their workforce will adopt the technology and how clients of their services will perceive their adoption of AI technologies. To overcome these challenges, AI developers need to co-design algorithms with clinicians and proactively undertake clinical trials to test the efficacy of their applications. AI companies and healthcare organizations also need to have an education and marketing strategy to inform public/patients about the benefits of adopting AI technologies.

I outline the above concerns largely to respond to the misconceptions and overhyping of AI by media and those who are not completely conversant with the mechanics behind AI applications. Overhyping AI affects the acceptability of AI especially if it leads to the adoption of immature or untested AI technologies. **However, there is much to lose healthcare organizations rule out adoption of AI technologies.** AI technologies can be of immense help in healthcare delivery:

- where complex data (clinical and financial) accumulates beyond the analytical capabilities of humans,
- where recurrent costs are blowing up healthcare budgets,
- where the computational ability of AI programs can uncover clinical patterns that humans may miss,
- where AI prowess can mitigate medical errors that are a product of human constraints,
- where current advances in computational resources and algorithms can identify new/novel drug treatments,
- where AI population health/surveillance programs can prevent the emergence of epidemics,
- when barriers for access to specialized medicine exist because of lengthy periods involved in training human clinicians and
- when intelligent communication and medical support devices can enhance the quality of senior citizens.

Imagine all this lost because of scepticism and resistance to adoption of AI technologies. Therefore, it is important that AI developers work with end-users in the development phases of AI applications and AI companies work with the media and relevant others in containing the hype and relaying realistic information about the capabilities of AI technologies. On the other hand, healthcare organizations and clinicians need to be open to what benefits AI adoption can bring to their services or they may be at the margins of a society where AI-assisted living has become the norm.

# Chapter 12: The case of AI medical software regulation in developing countries

Medical software is defined as the use of software for medical purposes. The uptake of medical software in healthcare has increased in line with increased application computation in healthcare delivery. Examples of medical software include software used in bedside monitors, MRIs, PACs, radiation therapy software, infusion pump rate devices, smartphone-based health applications. Etc. The *International Electrotechnical Commission* considers medical software as any software system that is developed for the purposed of use in a medical device or itself as a medical device. So, there is a clear linkage between medical devices and medical software. Yet, the understanding of what is medical software and how it should be regulated is unsatisfactory in developing countries. While there has been a considerable improvement in the way medical devices are regulated in developing countries, there hasn't been any serious deliberation of how medical software should be regulated in these contexts.

The emergence of AI software, in particular, deep learning, as a resource to aid clinical decision and in some instances automate clinical interpretation has created options for healthcare delivery unlike before. With demonstrated successes in medical imaging interpretation and disease screening, deep learning software has the potential for improving access to healthcare delivery in areas where there is limited or no specialised medical workforce. This ability hasn't escaped the attention of hospital groups, and entrepreneurs alike in developing countries. As low-cost computing and mobile data plans and better processes of data collection get established in developing countries, they also provide a platform for training and deploying AI medical software. Software that can have a significant beneficial impact on patient outcomes. Yet, the frameworks to regulate the use of such software is missing. Without such regulation, the ethical, legal and equity issues that many commentators have identified with unregulated use of AI medical software can lead to unfortunate consequences for the target communities.

Using India as an example of a developing country, we observe both the government and software developers have quickly identified the potential for use of AI in many sectors including healthcare. In recent years, many examples have emerged where technology companies have partnered with private hospital groups to incorporate AI medical software in routine clinical delivery. Also, entrepreneurs with flagship AI medical software products have raised millions of dollars leveraging the buzz around AI. Yet, it isn't clear in these instances how these applications have received necessary ethical and regulatory approvals and whether there are monitoring frameworks are in place to ensure the safety and privacy of patients.

Relative to many developing countries, the state of regulation of medical devices in India is advanced. With the Medical Devices Rules 2017, an improvement on the Drugs and Cosmetics Rule of 1945, there has been streamlining of how medical devices will be approved and regulated in India. These measures have enabled better harmonisation of Indian regulatory standards with medical device regulatory standards in developed countries. Yet, India falls behind countries such as the US and Australia in terms of medical software regulation. Medical software regulation is highly advanced in these countries. In particular, the US has been a world leader in setting out AI medical software regulatory policies. Its Food and Drug Administration (FDA) has laid out a road map as to how AI medical software will be approved and its ongoing use monitored in the US. The purpose of these FDA regulations is not to restrict the entry of AI medical software in the market but rather to facilitate entry of appropriate AI products in the market and to ensure both the interests of the software developers and patients are protected.

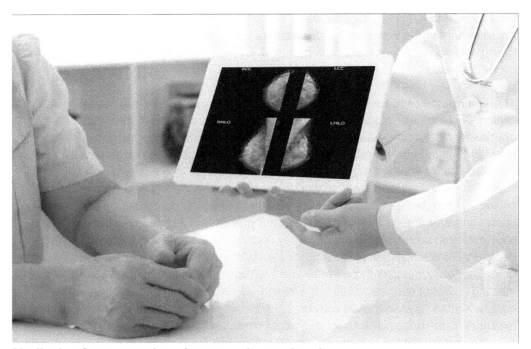

*Medical software needs to be properly regulated*

As there is significant interest in India regarding the use of AI in healthcare delivery, it becomes all the more important that appropriate arrangements guide the entry and use of AI medical software in the market. To enable this the Central Drugs Standard Control Organisation (which currently acts as the National Regulatory Authority for medical devices in India) can coordinate medical software regulation as other national regulatory authorities in developed countries such as the US FDA and Australian Therapeutic Goods Administration do. Also, customised AI medical software regulatory processes need to be issued similar to what FDA has attempted. Further, it is important that the data acquisition and utilisation process for developing commercial AI medical software is appropriately monitored through relevant regulatory mechanisms. In addition, the government should guide AI medical software developers to incorporate ethical measures in all aspects of their software development and testing. At this stage, these measures aren't in place, but we continue to see reports of the use of AI medical software in various aspects of healthcare delivery. Therefore, is important that the Indian government intervenes to establish appropriate regulatory arrangements not only to protect the interest of the consumer but also ensure the benefits of AI in healthcare are appropriately derived.

While the above narration relates to India, parallels can be found in many other developing countries where the AI medical software is being rolled out without regulatory arrangements to ensure appropriate use. A case of the cart being placed in front of the horse.

# The Promise

# Chapter 13: Will AI be the engine of healthcare in the future?

**It is 2035.** You are in a meeting in your office when you develop a sharp upper right chest pain radiating to your left arm. You pick up your mobile and dial a government authorised health emergency number. You are greeted by an AI-powered virtual assistant, who through analysis of your voice and breathing, and by looking into your past medical records suspects an unstable angina. The AI assistant then intelligently matches you to your dedicated healthcare provider and gets them to onto the call. You are then asked by the provider's virtual nurse to use a point of care cardiac troponin test kit with the assistance of your colleagues. The testing relays the results wirelessly to your healthcare provider who sets things in motion.

You are then airlifted to your provider hospital, where you are prepped for cardiac catheterisation. The catheterisation indicates over 70% stenosis of the proximal left anterior descending artery with a recommendation for a coronary artery bypass graft. You are then taken to the operating theatre to have this procedure. In both of these procedures, autonomous surgical robots have been key with a cardiac specialist providing oversight. In the postoperative phase, AI enabled monitoring devices and robot assistants progress you through to recovery. Remarkably, throughout this episode, the role of human clinicians has been very limited. Too hard to believe. Maybe not so unbelievable if we chart the progress of AI.

We all are using AI technologies in our lives like search engines, spam filters, voice assistants but very few of us are using AI enabled medical applications. It is my purpose to introduce some of them to you today. The most common area in medicine where AI is used is in data management. As medical data gets more complex, computational analysis becomes necessary. AI applications can help with the management of patient records and their analysis. In the Netherlands where 97 per cent of health records are digital, hospitals use Vektis intelligence to sift through data to highlight mistakes in treatments and identify gaps in clinical protocols so patient complications are avoided. With reading medical images like CT, MRI and X-ray images, AI had made tremendous leaps. In many instances, AI software has exceeded the accuracy of radiologists in making a diagnosis. AI enabled software now also provide health screening. In the UK, by using a combination of machine learning and speech recognition, the *Babylon* application provides a differential diagnosis and refers you to a human clinician where necessary. Another example of digital health assistance is *Sensely* Virtual Nurse that is available in the US. *Sensely* helps with monitoring of chronic disease patients by providing medication reminders and recommending a follow-up visit to doctors.

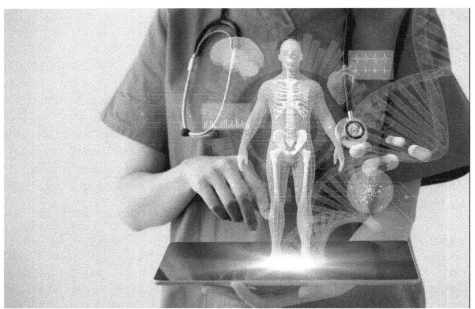

*AI applications will drive healthcare delivery in the future*

Talking of medication adherence. Medication Adherence is a big issue whereby studies indicate over 50 per cent of patients do not comply with treatment regimens. How do you get patients to comply with medicine intake? *Aicure*, an AI-enabled mobile app, provides a solution. By downloading the app and following the instructions the app provides, it has been found in studies of Hepatitis C and TB patients (where there are long drug regimens) there has been 100 % treatment completion rates. AI is also being used for drug creation. Developing drugs is a costly business because of the time and resources involved to identify the right drug molecules. *Atomwise* is an AI application that can make this process faster and cheaper. By using deep learning technology, *Atomwise* helps in the discovery of novel small molecules. In the Ebola epidemic that occurred some years ago, Atomwise identified a drug candidate that human scientists hadn't thought of using. Atomwise is now being used by leading pharmaceutical companies like *Merck* for new drug development. The final application I would like to talk about is in Surgery. As of now we only have robotic assistants being used in surgery. You may be familiar with *Davinci* robotic assistants being used for cardiac bypass and prostatectomy. However, we don't have an autonomous robot, which can operate without the direct involvement of a surgeon. This is changing though. *University of Washington* researchers are working on the 'Raven' surgical robot, which through a combination of new instrumentation, image fusion and biomarkers is able to perform minor surgeries on its own.

Now that we have discussed current medical applications of AI, going into the future how would an AI augmented Health System look like? AI will support administrative activities through automation of data collection and by aiding health data analysis. The analysis will ,in turn, support medical diagnosis and prediction. You will also see increased use of Robotic Assistants in areas where currently patient care assistants, nurses and allied health professionals are contributing. In the examination room, doctors will be employing AI apps and devices to diagnose medical conditions and also NLP enabled apps will be taking notes leaving more time for the doctor to examine the patient. There will also be autonomous robot surgery like the scenario I described at the beginning of this presentation. At the population and corporate level, AI will assist in identifying population groups at high risk of chronic diseases, assist with containing infectious disease spread and help in developing new medications faster. For elderly citizens, the advent of driverless transport, robotic assistants and AI monitoring devices means their quality of life and longevity will increase.

Further advances in quantum computing and Brain-Computer Interface technology will boost the capabilities of AI and its application in various aspects of healthcare. Quantum Computing utilises subatomic particles that can exist in more than one state at a time to overcome limitations with computing ability of traditional binary computers. Quantum computers will be able to undertake calculations and analysis in seconds that regular computers would take years. By using quantum computers, machine learning can be performed at advanced speeds. From a health perspective, this ability to review and analyse medical data can aid speedier and more accurate clinical decision making. Even leading to the possibility of autonomous AI clinical agents. Brain-Computer Interface converts neuronal information from the brain to commands that can be read by computers. This type of technology is useful in patients who cannot communicate through regular speech, say for example stroke victims, but use computers to convey information. The technology could also be used by stroke or disable patients to manipulate robotic support structures to perform manual tasks they normally can't. AI will be able to assist with the interpretation and analysis of the neuronal signals and convert them into computer- readable data.

While we can't accurately predict how healthcare will be delivered in 2035, we can make an educated guess that it will be most certainly driven by technologies like AI, Quantum Computing, Robotics, Brain-Computer-Interfaces amongst other technologies. So, what will be the role of human clinicians in this system? That is discussed in the next chapter.

# Chapter 14: The role of human clinicians in an automated health system

Eric Topol, a Professor of Genomics and Cardiologist, in his 2015 NYTimes bestseller '*The Patient Will See You Now*', foresees the demise of the current form of hospital-based acute care delivery (with a shift to delivery of care at homes of patients) along with replacement of human delivered clinical services by smart systems/devices in the coming future. I would not dare to predict the replacement of human clinicians but can easily foresee the automation of a large part of human-led clinical care in the coming decades.

Healthcare has been a fertile domain for computational intelligence researchers to apply AI techniques including artificial neural networks, evolutionary computing, expert systems and natural language processing. The rise in interest and investment in AI research has coincided with the increasing release of AI driven clinical applications. Many of these applications have automated the three key cornerstones of medical care: diagnosis, prognosis and therapy. So, it is not hard to see why commentators, including clinical commentators, are predicting the replacement of human clinicians by AI systems.

While it is indeed rational, based on current trends in AI research, to imagine automation of many human clinician (for convenience sake, I am focusing on physicians rather than other professions such as nurses, allied health professionals) led tasks including interpretation of laboratory and imaging results (AI applications are already matching the radiologist's accuracy in interpretation of MRI, CT and Radiological images), predicting clinical outcomes (AI applications have successfully predicted acute conditions by reviewing both structured and unstructured patient data) and diagnosing various acute conditions (in fact the earliest AI applications, dating back to the '70s, already had this ability); it is hard to imagine AI systems completely replacing human clinicians in conveying diagnosis and discussing complex treatment regimens with patients, especially with high risk patients. There are some other areas where it is equally hard to foresee automation of clinical tasks such as some complex procedures and making final treatment decisions. So, what is to come?

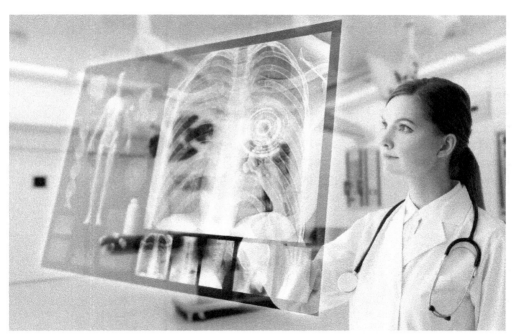

*AI agents will cohabit with human clinicians in delivering healthcare in the future*

I foresee a cohabitation model. A model that accepts the inevitable automation of a significant number of tasks that are currently performed by human clinicians (the at-risk areas are where there is less human interaction and where there is a structured process in implementing the task; structure means algorithms can be developed easier you see) but allows for human clinicians to make the final decision and be the lead communicator with patients.

# Chapter 15: Why a third AI winter is unlikely to occur?

Around the late 1970s, the so-called first 'AI winter' emerged because of technical limitations ( the failure of machine translation and connectionism to achieve their objectives). Then after in the late 1980s, the second AI winter occurred because of financial/economic reasons (DARPA cutbacks, restriction on new spending in academic environments and collapse of the LISP machine market). With the current re-emergence of AI and the increasing attention being paid to it by governments and corporates, some are speculating another AI winter may occur.

*Will another AI winter occur?*

What these commentators don't take into account is the conditions that prevailed in the late '70s and '80s are not the conditions prevalent now. The current demand for AI has emerged because of actual needs (the need to compute massive amounts of data). With the rapid rise in computational power, increase in acquisition of data from all quarters of life, increased investment by governments and corporates, dedicated research units both in academia and corporate bodies, integration with other innovative IT areas like IoT, Robotics, AR, VR, Brain-Machine Interfaces..etc **there has never been a better time for AI** to flourish. What sceptics seem to mistakenly assume is that developers are intending for Artificial General Intelligence to occur. Maybe there is a time when this is to occur but nearly all developers are focused on developing narrow AI applications. The rediscovery of the usefulness of early machine learning algorithms and introduction of newer forms of machine learning algorithms like convolutional neural networks, GANs, Deep Q networks..etc coupled with advances in the understanding of symbolism, neurobiology, causation and correlational theories have advanced the progress of AI applications. If commentators stop expecting that AI systems will replace all human activities and understand that AI is best suited to augment/enhance/support human activity, there would be less pessimism about the prospects of AI. Of course, there will be failures as AI gets applied in various industries followed by the inevitable 'I told you so' by arm-chair commentators or sardonic academics but this will not stop the progress of AI and related systems. On the other hand, if AI researchers and developers can aim for realistic objectives and invite scrutiny of their completed applications, the waffle from the cynics can be put to rest.

So where does this leave health services and the application of AI in healthcare? Traditionally the clinical workforce has been slow adopters of technological innovations. This is expected as errors and risks in clinical care unlike other industries are less tolerated and many times unacceptable. However, the greatest promise for AI is in its application in healthcare. For long, health systems across the world have been teetering on financial bankruptcy with governments or other entities bailing them out (I can't think of a health system, which runs on substantial profits) . A main component of the costs of running health services is recurrent costs, which includes recurrent administrative and workforce costs. Governments or policy wonks have never been able to come up with a solution to address this except reiterate the tired mantra of early prevention or advocate for deficit plugging or suggest new models of workforce, which are hard to implement. Coupled with this scenario, is the humongous growth in medical information that no ordinary clinician can retain and pass onto their patients or include in their treatment, rapid introduction of newer forms of drugs and treatments and the unfortunate increase in the number of medical errors (In the US, approximately 251,454 deaths are caused per annum due to medical errors).

AI Technology provides an appropriate solution to address these issues considering the potential of AI enabled clinical decision support systems, digital scribes, medical chatbots, electronic health records, medical image analysers, surgical robots, surveillance systems; all of which can be developed and delivered at economical pricing. Of course, a fully automated health service is many years away and AI regulatory and assessment frameworks are yet to be properly instituted. So, we won't be realising the full potential of AI in healthcare in the immediate future. However, if health services and clinicians think AI is another fad like Betamax, Palm Pilots, Urine therapy, Bloodletting and lobotomies they are very mistaken. The number of successful instances of the application of AI in healthcare delivery is increasing at a rapid rate for it to be a flash in the pan. Also, many governments including the Chinese, UAE, UK and French governments have prioritised the application of AI in healthcare delivery and continue to invest in its growth. While AI technology will never replace human clinicians, it will most certainly replace clinicians and health service providers who do not learn about it or engage with it. Therefore, it is imperative for health service providers, medical professional bodies, medical schools and health departments to actively incorporate AI/technology (machine learning, robotics and expert systems) in their policies and strategies. If not, it will be a scenario of too little and too late depriving patients of the immense benefits of personalised and cost-efficient care that AI enabled health systems can deliver.

# Chapter 16: AI in Healthcare-Are we there yet?

With regard to AI in Healthcare, one could be mistaken that the entry of AI in healthcare is inevitable. Recent developments include two major studies, where machine learning classifiers used for hypothetico-deductive reasoning were found to be as accurate as paediatricians and the other where a deep-learning based automated algorithm outperformed thoracic radiologists in accuracy and was externally validated in multiple sites. The former study is significant in that machine learning classifiers are now proven to be not only useful for medical imaging interpretation but also useful in extracting clinically relevant information from electronic patient records. The latter study is also significant in that the algorithm could detect multiple abnormalities in chest x-rays (useful in real-world settings) and was validated multiple times using external data-sets. Coupled with these developments, we now have the FDA gearing up for the inevitable use of AI software in clinical practice by developing a draft framework anticipating modifications to AI medical software. Also, we now have medical professional bodies across the world welcoming the entry of AI in medicine albeit cautiously and by issuing guidelines. Compared to even a year ago, it seems AI has definitely had a resounding impact on healthcare. Even the venerable Institute of Electrical and Electronic Engineers is tracking where AI is exceeding the performance of clinicians:
https://spectrum.ieee.org/static/ai-vs-doctors
However, I most certainly think we have yet to see the proper entry of AI in healthcare. Let me explain why and what needs to be done to enable this?

While there is strong evidence emerging about the usefulness of machine learning, especially neural networks in interpreting multiple medical modalities, the generalization of such successes is relatively uncommon. While there has been progress with the ability to minimize generalization error (through avoidance of over-fitting) and understanding how generalization and optimization of neural networks work, it still remains the fact that prediction of class labels outside trained data sets is not for certain. In medicine, this means deep learning algorithms that have shown success in certain contexts are not guaranteed to deliver the same success even with similar data in a different context. There is also the causal probabilistic approach of current machine learning algorithms, which do not necessarily align with the causal deterministic model of diagnostic medicine (I have covered this issue in Chapter 5). Even if we accept that machine learning/deep learning models with current limitations are useful in healthcare, there is the fact there is limited readiness of hospitals/health services to deploy these models in clinical practice. The lack of readiness spans infrastructure, policies/guidelines and education. Also, governments and regulatory bodies in many countries don't have specific policies and regulatory frameworks to guide the application of AI in healthcare. So, what has to be done?

As illustrated below, the following steps have to be adopted for us to see AI bloom in the healthcare context.

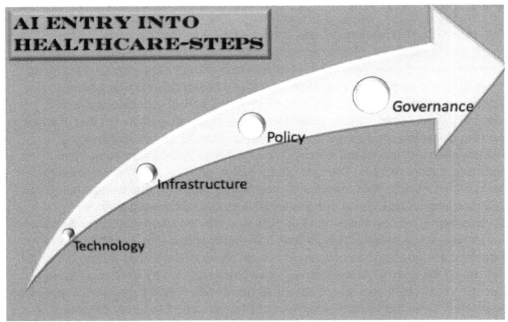

*Steps required for entry and use of AI in Healthcare*

The first step is the development and use of appropriate AI **Technology** in Medicine. This means ensuring there are validity and relevance of the algorithms being used to address the healthcare issues. For example, if a *convolutional neural network* model has shown success in screening *pulmonary tuberculosis* through chest x-ray interpretation it doesn't necessarily mean it is equipped to identify other chest x-ray abnormalities say *atelectasis* or *pneumothorax*. So, the model should be used for the exact purpose it was trained. Also, the model trained with a labelled x-ray data-set from a particular region has to be validated with a data-set from another region and context. Another issue that pertains to technology is the type of machine learning model being used. While deep learning seems to be in vogue, it is not necessarily appropriate in all medical contexts. Because of the limitations it poses with explainability, other machine learning models like Decision Trees, which lend themselves to interpretability should be considered.

The second step in facilitating the entry and establishment of AI in healthcare is **Infrastructure**. What do I mean by infrastructure? At this stage, even in developed countries, hospitals do not necessarily have digital platforms and data warehouse structures for machine learning models to successfully operate. Many hospitals are still grappling with the roll-out of electronic health records. This platform will be essential for machine learning algorithms to mine and query patient data. Also, to train many machine learning models structured data is necessary (some models can work on unstructured data as this application). This data structuring process includes data labelling and creating data warehouses. Not all hospitals, facing budget crunches, have this infrastructure/capability. Further, the clinical and administrative workforce and patient community are to be educated about AI (if AI applications will be used in clinical practice and healthcare delivery). How many healthcare organizations have this infrastructure readiness? I doubt many. So infrastructural issues are most certainly to be addressed before one can think of the use of AI in the healthcare context.

The next step, **Policy**, is also critical. Policy covers both governmental and institutional strategies to guide the deployment of AI for healthcare delivery, and regulatory frameworks to facilitate the entry of and regulate AI medical software in the market. There is definitely progress here with many governments, national regulatory bodies, medical professional bodies and think tanks issuing guidance about this matter. Yet, there are gaps in that many of these guidance documents are theoretical or cursory in nature or not linked to existing infrastructure. Worse yet, is in countries where such policies and guidance don't exist at all. Also, an issue is limited funding mechanisms to support AI research and commercialization, which has significantly hampered innovation or indigenous development of AI medical applications.

The final step that needs to be considered is **Governance**. This step not only covers the regulation frameworks at the national level (necessary to scrutinize and validate AI applications) but also monitoring and evaluation frameworks at the institutional level. It also covers the requirement to mitigate the risk involved in the application of AI in clinical care and the need to create patient-centric AI models. The latter two steps are vital in clinical governance and continuous quality improvement. Many institutions have issued ethical guidelines for the application of AI in Healthcare, but I am yet to see clinical governance models for the use of AI in clinical care. It is critical that clinical governance models for the application of AI in healthcare delivery are developed.

Addressing the steps, I list above: *Technology, Infrastructure, Policy* and *Governance* appropriately will most certainly facilitate the entry and establishment of AI in Healthcare. Also, with the accelerated developments in AI technology and increasing interest in AI by policymakers, clinical bodies and healthcare institutions, maybe we are not that far away from seeing this occur.

# Index